Ancient Egypt

Written by Alex Raynham
Illustrated by Victor Tavares

The beautiful Nile

The Nile is the longest river in Africa. It goes through nine countries before it reaches Egypt. Most of Egypt is a desert, but the Nile Valley is beautiful and green. Today, 95% of Egyptians live along the Nile.

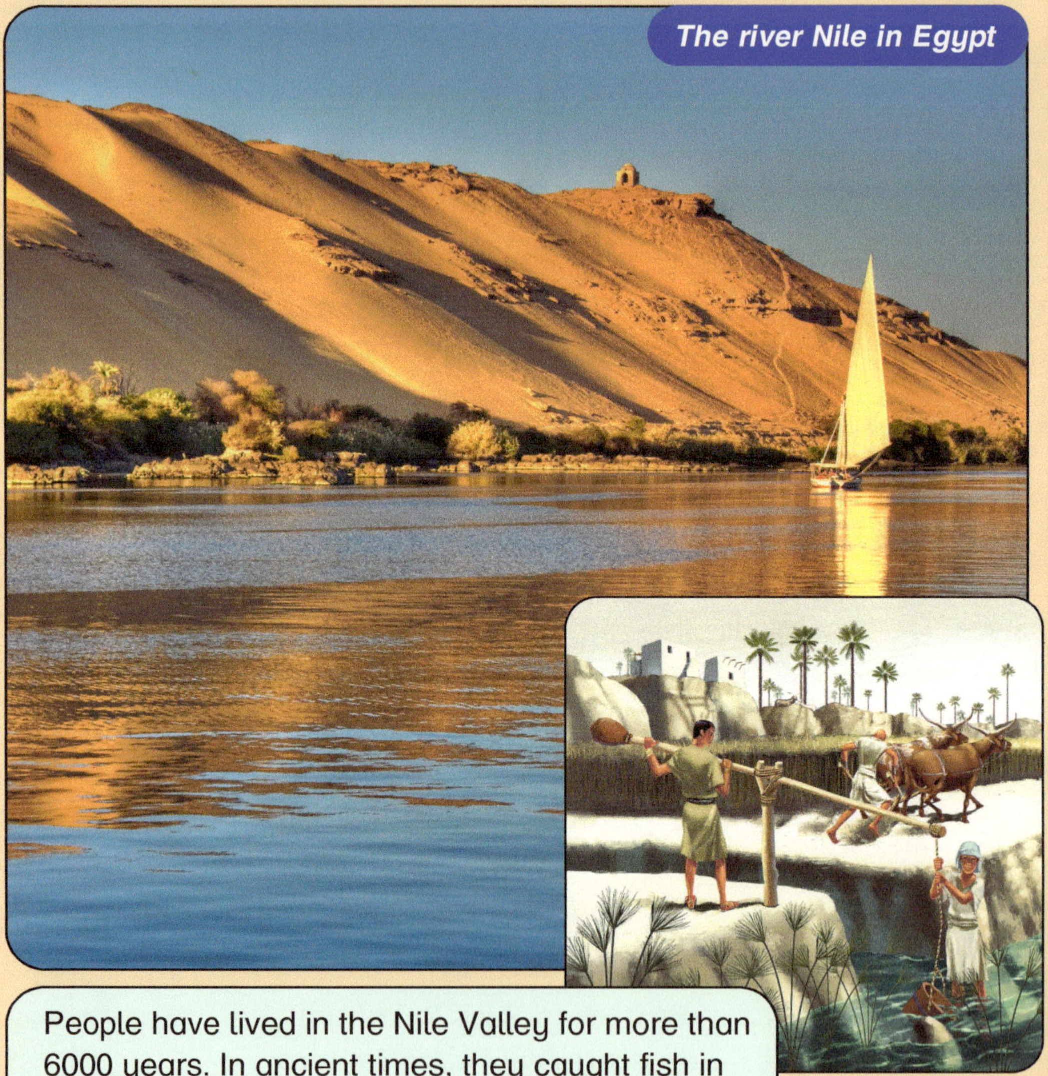

The river Nile in Egypt

People have lived in the Nile Valley for more than 6000 years. In ancient times, they caught fish in the river, kept animals and grew plants for food.

Tall plants grew along the Nile. The ancient Egyptians used flax plants to make cloth for clothes. They used papyrus plants to make beautiful boats. The boats travelled up and down the Nile, from the Mediterranean Sea to the middle of Africa.

Every year, in the summer, the Nile flooded. After the flood, there was more mud in the Nile Valley. The ancient Egyptians used the mud to grow plants and to make bricks. They built houses with the bricks.

Pharaohs

About 5000 years ago, north and south Egypt had different kings. Then a king called Narmer won a battle and became the first pharaoh – the ruler of all Egypt.

The pharaohs ruled Egypt for 3000 years. Most people in Egypt were poor farmers, but the pharaohs lived in beautiful palaces. They had lots of slaves, too.

Narmer built Egypt's first capital city next to the Nile at Memphis.

There were many great pharaohs, like Queen Hatshepsut and King Rameses the Second.

Hatshepsut, 1508–1458 BC

Hatshepsut ruled Egypt for 22 years. Most pharaohs were men, so Hatshepsut wore men's clothes and a man's beard! A lot of pharaohs fought with other countries, but Hatshepsut traded with other countries. As a result, Egypt became rich.

Rameses the Great, 1303–1213 BC

Rameses the Second was 20 when he became the pharaoh and he ruled Egypt for more than 60 years. He built many cities and temples, and Egypt became a big empire. People call him Rameses the Great.

Amazing Fact
Rameses the Great had more than 100 children!

Temples

The ancient Egyptians built large stone temples for their gods. Many of them are still there today. Hatshepsut built a huge temple because she wanted people to remember her for ever.

Hatshepsut's temple is about 3500 years old, but it looks new.

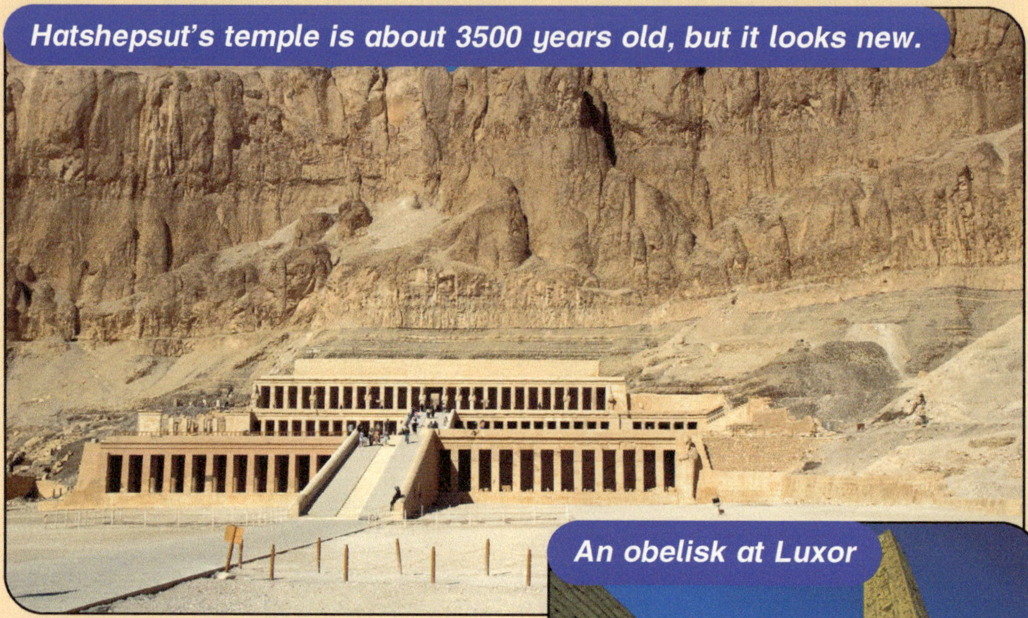

An obelisk at Luxor

The ancient Egyptians put tall stone monuments outside some temples. The monuments are called obelisks. They have writing and pictures on them to tell people about the gods and pharaohs.

Amazing Fact

Rameses the Great built two huge obelisks at the temple in Luxor. Each obelisk weighed over 250 tonnes!

Mummies

When important Egyptians died, people made their bodies into mummies. This kept the body safe. Now we can tell what they looked like when they were alive.

An Egyptian mummy in a coffin

People called embalmers made the mummies. It took about 70 days to make a mummy.

- First the embalmers took the organs out of the body and put them into special jars. They pulled the brain out through the nose!
- Then the embalmers used salts to dry the body.
- Next they wrapped the body in cloth.
- Finally they put the mummy into a beautiful coffin.

An organ jar

Pyramids

The ancient Egyptians buried the mummies of the pharaohs in pyramids. There are more than 130 pyramids in Egypt. The oldest pyramid is at Saqqara. It is nearly 4700 years old.

The oldest pyramid, at Saqqara

The Great Pyramid of Khufu, at Giza

The biggest pyramid is the Great Pyramid, at Giza. It was built for the pharaoh Khufu. It is more than 4500 years old. It is 147 metres high. For nearly 4000 years it was the tallest building in the world!

It took many years to build a pyramid. There are over two million stones in the Great Pyramid of Khufu. Boats carried the stones down the Nile to Giza. The biggest stones weighed 80 tonnes, and they came from Aswan – 800 kilometres away! Hundreds of people pulled the stones to the top of the pyramid.

Some of the builders were slaves, but many were not. They didn't work every day, and the pharaoh built houses for them.

Amazing Fact

At Giza, there are three pyramids and a huge statue of a sphinx. A sphinx is a mythical animal with a lion's body and a pharaoh's head.

The Valley of the Kings

In about 1800 BC, the ancient Egyptians stopped building pyramids. They started to build tombs for the pharaohs and important people. They built the tombs in a valley near the Nile – the Valley of the Kings.

The Valley of the Kings, at Luxor

Many tombs were full of treasure. Robbers tried to get into them, but it wasn't easy! The tombs were deep underground and they had secret doors. Curses on the walls said, 'Don't open this tomb – bad things will happen to you.'

Inside an Egyptian tomb

Tutankhamun

In 1922, a British archeologist called Howard Carter found the tomb of the pharaoh Tutankhamun. The tomb was full of amazing treasure, like a gold bed and a beautiful gold mask.

Howard Carter by Tutankhamun's tomb

Tutankhamun's mask

After Howard Carter found the tomb, many of his friends died. So people wrote stories in the newspapers and made horror films about the curse of Tutankhamun.

Amazing Fact

Tutankhamun only ruled Egypt for nine years and he was only 19 when he died.

What did the ancient Egyptians like?

People in ancient Egypt loved music and dancing. They also liked jewellery and nice clothes. Men and women used make-up, and rich women wore pretty shoes.

The ancient Egyptians made beautiful pictures and statues. They also wrote stories. One story was about a poor girl, a pharaoh and a pair of shoes. It became the story *Cinderella*.

Egyptian shoes

An Egyptian statue

Writing

The ancient Egyptians made paper from papyrus plants and they used pens. Most Egyptians didn't know how to read or write – that was the job of the scribes.

Egyptian hieroglyphs

There were different types of writing in ancient Egypt. One type used pictures called hieroglyphs. For many years archeologists didn't understand hieroglyphs. But in 1799, some French soldiers found a stone near Rosetta. There was Greek and Egyptian writing on the stone. A Frenchman read the Greek words and they helped him to translate the hieroglyphs. It wasn't easy – it took 23 years!

Ancient Egyptian books were written on a long piece of paper called a scroll.

The end of ancient Egypt

Ancient Egypt ended in 30 BC when Egypt became part of the Roman Empire. Today, millions of tourists visit the ruins of ancient Egyptian temples and pyramids, and archeologists find more ruins all the time.

Ancient Egyptian pens

Amazing Fact

In 2011, archeologists found 17 more ancient pyramids in Egypt!

The ancient Egyptians used many things we use today, like pens, scissors, locks, keys and calendars.

The Book of Thoth

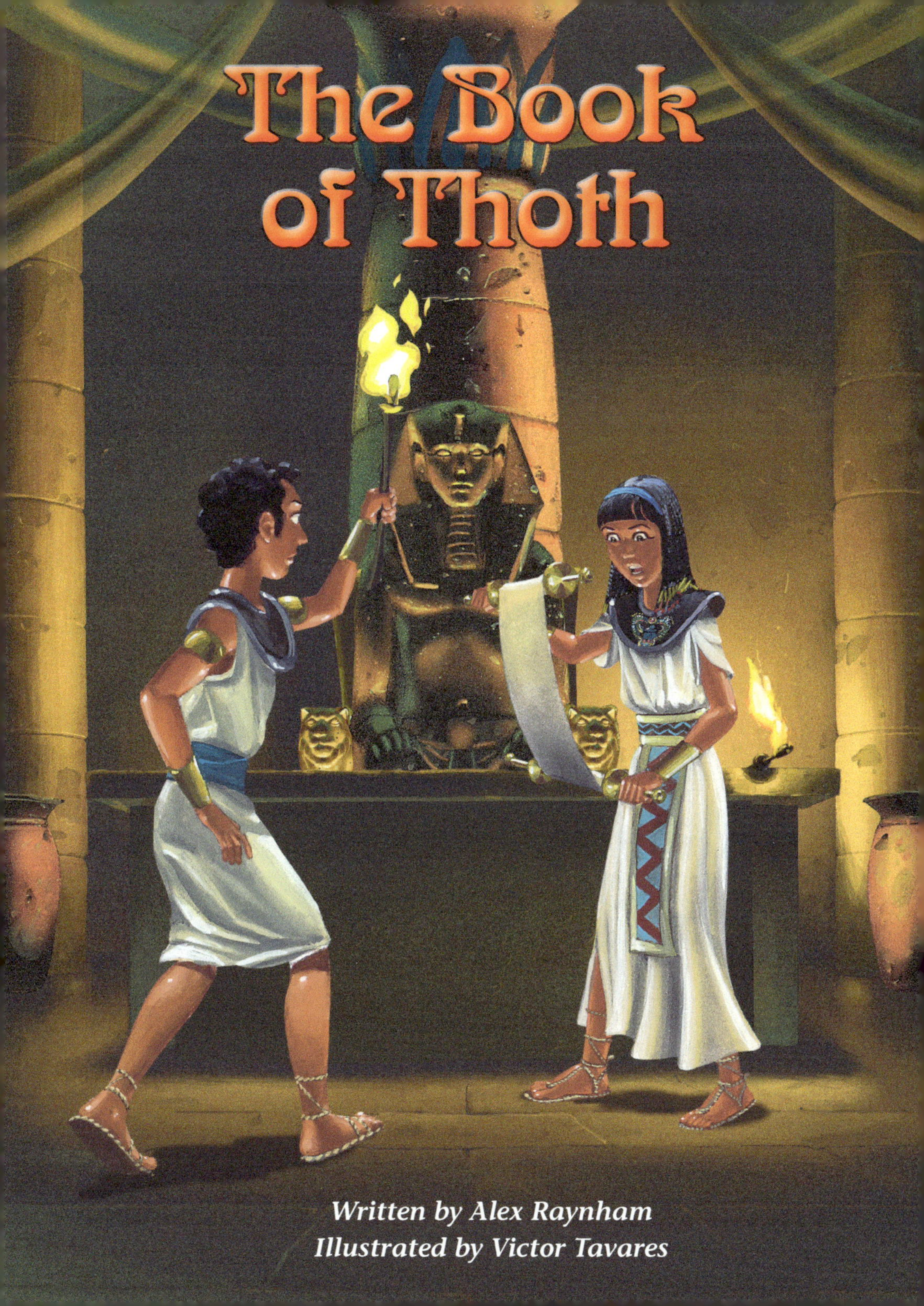

Written by Alex Raynham
Illustrated by Victor Tavares

Prince Setne is the oldest son of the pharaoh. He lives with his brothers and sisters in a beautiful palace by the river Nile. But it isn't easy being a prince.
Wake up, great prince. You've got an archery lesson and a riding lesson this morning.
Oh no! I can't do archery and I can't ride a horse!

The pharaoh watches the children's archery lesson. Princess Nefertari can shoot well, but the pharaoh is worried because her brother Setne is terrible.
Setne can't shoot well, but he's going to be a pharaoh one day!
Nefertari can help him. They can practise together.

Setne is happy that Nefertari is helping him, but he doesn't want anyone in the palace to know. So they go across the Nile in a boat to practise archery.
Oh no! I missed.
Come on – let's go and find your arrow.

The children look for Setne's arrow, but they find a tomb!
Let's go inside.
But it's dark!
It's OK. We can use the torches.
They light the torches and go into the tomb.
They find a beautiful golden room. There is a scroll on a stone table. Nefertari opens it and reads, 'This is the Book of Thoth. Read it and you will know everything.'
Great! Let's take the book.
No – there's a curse! It says, 'Don't take the book from this tomb – terrible things will happen.'

But Setne wants to know everything. The book can help him to be a great prince, so he takes it. The children leave the golden room, then suddenly they stop.
Snakes! The tomb is full of snakes!
Snakes hate fire. Quick, use your torch!

The children run out of the tomb, but Nefertari is worried.
Take the book back! It's dangerous.
No! I want it. I want to be good at everything.

That night in the palace, Setne reads the Book of Thoth. He reads a story about a horse. Then he goes to bed and dreams about riding a horse.

The next day, Setne's parents watch his riding lesson. They are very happy.

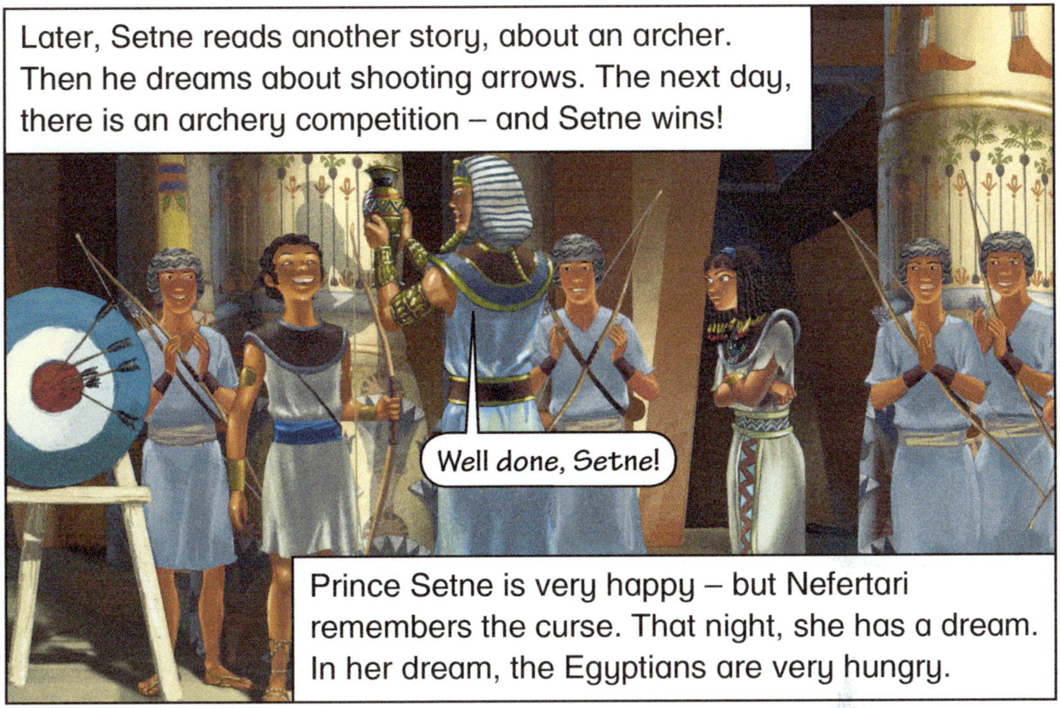
Later, Setne reads another story, about an archer. Then he dreams about shooting arrows. The next day, there is an archery competition – and Setne wins!
Well done, Setne!
Prince Setne is very happy – but Nefertari remembers the curse. That night, she has a dream. In her dream, the Egyptians are very hungry.

That summer, it is very hot and the flood is late. The river Nile is dry, so the farmers haven't got any water.
The flood is late.
My people are hungry.

Nefertari talks to her brother.
Remember the curse, Setne. Take the book back to the tomb. Then the flood can come.
No! The book helps me to be a great prince!

Nefertari is angry with Setne.
Don't be selfish! Great princes help their people.
That night, Setne dreams that it is raining and the valley is green again. There is water and food, and the people are happy. Setne knows the right thing to do.

In the morning, Setne rides across the dry river with the book. Nefertari watches him, then she goes to their parents.

Setne rides to the tomb. He is afraid, but he goes in. This time, there are no snakes.
He puts the Book of Thoth in the golden room.

When Setne comes out of the tomb, it is raining! Water, stones and mud are coming down the hill. They are closing the tomb.

Setne rides back across the Nile. But it is flooding fast and soon the water is very deep.
Come on!
Setne can't ride very well anymore because he hasn't got the book. But he holds onto the horse. Slowly, they cross the river.

In the village outside the palace, the people are very happy. They are laughing and shouting.
It's raining!
The Nile is flooding!
We aren't hungry now!

In the palace, Setne's family are waiting for him.
I took the book back to the tomb.
Yes! I told our parents all about the book.
My brave prince! You saved Egypt.
One day, you will be a great pharaoh.
Setne smiles. He doesn't need the Book of Thoth anymore.

Activities

1 Write the words in the table.

scribe arrow embalmer ~~pharaoh~~ tomb torch
farmer temple jar house mask palace

People	Things	Buildings
pharaoh		

2 Circle T (True) or F (False).

1	Most people in Egypt live in the desert.	T	(F)
2	The ancient Egyptians made boats out of plants.	T	F
3	The river Nile flooded every summer.	T	F
4	The ancient Egyptians made their houses out of stones.	T	F
5	The pharaohs ruled Egypt for 5000 years.	T	F
6	The first capital city of ancient Egypt was Memphis.	T	F
7	Obelisks are very small stones with writing on them.	T	F
8	Another name for Rameses the Second is Rameses the Great.	T	F

3 Put the sentences in order.

How to make a mummy

- [ ] Wrap the body.
- [ ] Use salts to dry the body.
- [1] Take the organs out of the body.
- [ ] Put the mummy in a coffin.
- [ ] Put a mask on the mummy's face.
- [ ] Put the organs into special jars.

4 Complete the crossword. Find the mystery word.

1

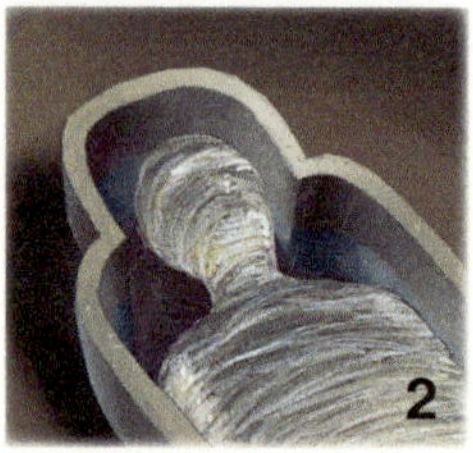
2

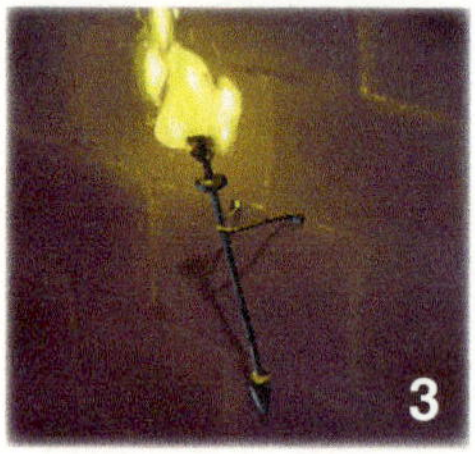
3

4

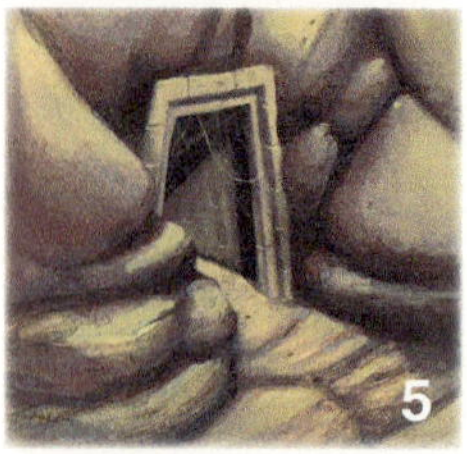
5

6

7

		1 p	a	p	y	r	u	s
2								
		3						
		4						
		5						
	6							
7								

The mystery word is ______________________ .

5 Answer the questions.

1 Why did Queen Hatshepsut wear a man's beard?

Most pharaohs were men.

2 Who built many cities and temples?

____

3 How long did it take to make a mummy?

____

4 How many pyramids are there in Egypt?

____

5 How did the pharaoh help the pyramid builders?

____

6 Where did the ancient Egyptians build tombs?

____

7 What did Howard Carter find in 1922?

____

8 What did some French soldiers find near Rosetta?

____

6 Circle the correct words.

1 Setne is the (*oldest*) / *youngest* son of the pharaoh.

2 Setne and Nefertari find a *mummy* / *book* inside a tomb.

3 There are *fish* / *snakes* inside the tomb.

4 After Setne *dreams* / *talks* about riding, he is very good.

5 That summer, the weather is very hot and the *winter* / *flood* is late.

6 Setne puts the book back in the *tomb* / *river*.

7 Look at the hieroglyphs. Then write the message in English.

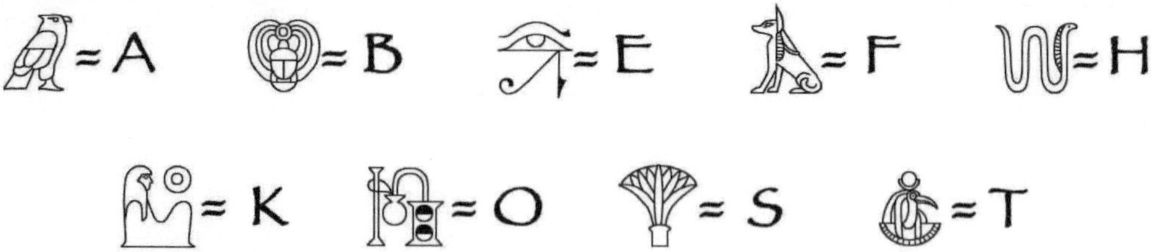

____

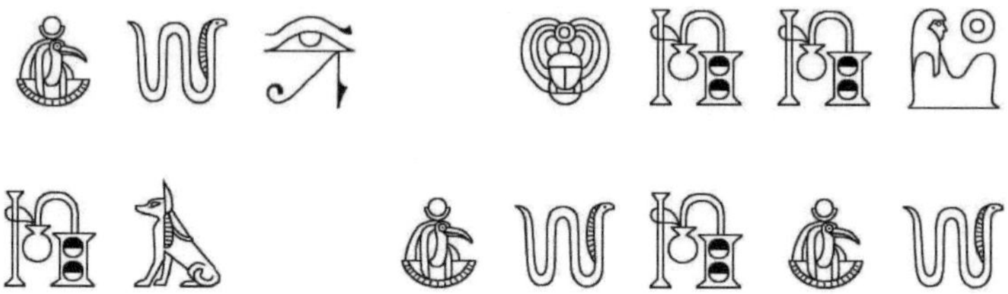

The message is: ____

8 Complete the summary of the story.

One day, Prince [1] Setne goes across the river with his [2] __________ Nefertari. They want to practise [3] __________ . They find a [4] __________ . Inside, Setne and Nefertari find a beautiful [5] __________ and a scroll. The scroll is called the Book of Thoth. There is a [6] __________ in the book. It says, 'Don't take the book!' But Setne takes the book and he [7] __________ it before he goes to bed. The book helps him to be good at archery and [8] __________ . But the floods are late and the people are very [9] __________ . So Setne rides back across the river Nile with the book. When he puts the book back in the tomb, it starts to [10] __________ . The river Nile floods and the people of Egypt are happy again.

Bilingual Dictionary

Key: (n) = noun (n pl) = plural noun
(v) = verb (adj) = adjective

Write the words in your language.

ancient (adj) ____________________
archeologist (n) ____________________
archery (n) ____________________
arrow (n) ____________________
battle (n) ____________________
beard (n) ____________________
brain (n) ____________________
brave (adj) ____________________
brick (n) ____________________
buried, to bury (v) ____________________
calendar (n) ____________________
cloth (n) ____________________
competition (n) ____________________
curse (n) ____________________
deep (adj) ____________________
desert (n) ____________________
dream (n, v) ____________________
dry (adj) ____________________
embalmer (n) ____________________
empire (n) ____________________
flood (n, v) ____________________
god (n) ____________________
gold (n) ____________________
horror film (n) ____________________
hungry (adj) ____________________
jewellery (n) ____________________
lock and key (n) ____________________
make-up (n) ____________________
mask (n) ____________________
monument (n) ____________________
mud (n) ____________________
mythical (adj) ____________________
organ (n) ____________________
palace (n) ____________________
poor (adj) ____________________
practise (v) ____________________
prince (n) ____________________
ride (a horse) (v) ____________________
river (n) ____________________
robber (n) ____________________
ruins (n pl) ____________________
ruler (n) ____________________
salt (n) ____________________
scroll (n) ____________________
secret (adj) ____________________
selfish (adj) ____________________
shoot (v) ____________________
slave (n) ____________________
snake (n) ____________________
soldier (n) ____________________
stone (n) ____________________
temple (n) ____________________
tomb (n) ____________________
torch (n) ____________________
traded, to trade (v) ____________________
translate (v) ____________________
treasure (n) ____________________
valley (n) ____________________
wrapped, to wrap (v) ____________________

Macmillan Education
4 Crinan Street
London N1 9XW
A division of Springer Nature Limited

Companies and representatives throughout the world

ISBN 978-1-3800-3842-5

Written by Alex Raynham
The author has asserted his right to be identified as the author of this work in accordance with the Copyright, Designs and Patents Act 1988.

First published 2014
This edition published 2019

Designed by Carolyn Gibson
Illustrated by Victor Tavares
Photo research by Victoria Gaunt
Cover photographs by Getty Images/E+/pidjoe (background), Pixtal.

The author and publishers would like to thank the following for permission to reproduce their photographs: **Alamy Stock Photo**/age fotostock p3, Alamy Stock Photo/IanDagnall Computing p7(l), Alamy Stock Photo/Michael Ventura p10(b), Alamy Stock Photo/ Leigh Prather p13(b), Alamy Stock Photo/Jon Bower Egypt p9, Alamy/Peter Horree p7(r), Alamy/imagebroker p5(l); **The Art Archive**/Egyptian Museum Cairo /Gianni Dagli Orti p12(l); **Getty Images**/Stuart Dee p1, Getty Images/Moment/Matt Champlin p2, Getty Images/De Agostini p4, Getty Images/Latitudestock p6(t), Getty Images/Smartshots International p8(b), Getty Images/antonbelo 10(t), Getty Images/Robert Harding Images p11(b), Getty Images/Egyptian p12(t), Getty Images/E+/pidjoe p13(t), Getty Images p14(t), Getty Images/SSPL p14(b); **Glow Images** p5(r); **Photoshot** p11(t), Photoshot/ Picture Alliance p12(bl), Photoshot/EUR p6(b), Photoshot/TIPS pp8(t).

Printed and bound in Brazil

2025
16